Four Seasons
of Corn

Four Seasons of Corn

WE ARE STILL HERE

NATIVE AMERICANS TODAY

A Winnebago
Tradition

by Sally M. Hunter • Photographs by Joe Allen

Lerner Publications Company ● Minneapolis

Series Editors: LeeAnne Engfer, Gordon Regguinti
Series Consultants: W. Roger Buffalohead, Juanita G. Corbine Espinosa

Acknowledgments
A special thank you to Anna Rae Funmaker of the Hochunk Historic Preservation
Department of the Wisconsin Hochunk Nation for her advice, proofreading, and
insights into the development of this manuscript.

Illustrations by Carly Bordeau

BAO   4/97   19.95

This book is available in two editions:
Library binding by Lerner Publications Company
Soft cover by First Avenue Editions
241 First Avenue North
Minneapolis, MN 55401

ISBN: 0-8225-2658-1 (lib. bdg.)
ISBN: 0-8225-9741-1 (pbk.)

LIBRARY OF CONGRESS CATALOGING-IN-PUBLICATION DATA

Hunter, Sally M.
     Four seasons of corn : a Winnebago tradition / by Sally M. Hunter;
  photographs by Joe Allen.
     Includes bibliographical references.
     Summary: Twelve-year-old Russell learns how to grow and dry corn
  from his Winnebago grandfather.
     ISBN 0-8225-2658-1 (hardcover : alk. paper). - ISBN 0-8225-9741-1
  (pbk. : alk. paper)
     1. Winnebago Indians—Food—Juvenile literature. 2. Winnebago
  Indians—Agriculture—Juvenile literature. 3. Corn—Social aspects—
  Juvenile literature. 4. Corn—Folklore. [1. Winnebago Indians—
  Food. 2. Indians of North America—Food. 3. Corn.] I. Allen,
  Joe, ill. II. Title.
  E99.W7H85 1997
  394.1'089975—dc2   96–17625

Manufactured in the United States of America
1 2 3 4 5 6 – JR – 02 01 00 99 98 97

This book is dedicated to Preston Thompson, an elder of the Eagle clan, for sharing his wisdom with the Hochunk children who will bring the traditions into the future.

Preface

I think it's great being an Indian grandmother in the city. I get to see my grandchildren often because they also live in the city. The quiet forests and lakes of our reservation homes seem far away when we are walking on concrete sidewalks and listening to the roar of traffic. In the city, our grandchildren are surrounded by non-Indians in school and everywhere else they go. But in our family we take care of one another by getting together often and having fun.

My husband and I belong to different Indian nations. He is Hochunk, and I am Anishinabe, or Ojibway. Having a mixed marriage is not a problem, because in both of our nations, the children belong to the clan of the father. So our children belong to the Hochunk Eagle Clan. We continue some Anishinabe customs, but most of our Indian traditions come from the Hochunk people. I think it is enriching for children to identify with more than one Indian and non-Indian culture. They have more choices in life.

We fill our big old house with family and guests for dinners, birthdays, and spiritual ceremonies. Sometimes we have a gathering every weekend. There is always teasing and laughing, because someone has funny stories or new adventures to share. And when we go to a powwow or ceremony, we pack the family in the van to drive to the reservation. Whenever we have the children together, we tell stories about our family life and the past. We want the kids to be proud of their achievements and of being Indian.

For almost 20 years, we have processed corn in our back-yard. We have been a curiosity to our neighbors! Now other families can share our story—this book will solve the mystery of what those Indian neighbors have been doing in the yard all these years. We are teaching our children to value the old ways as well as the modern.

In the spring, when the soil is ready, we begin the cycle of growing and processing corn once again. The soft, plowed soil under our feet and the smell of sweet lilacs make us feel close to the earth. We call the earth Mother because she provides food and medicines for her people. At first, our grandchildren feel out of place and unfamiliar with the countryside. In a few minutes, they relax and en-  joy the quiet, the warm soil, and the work. The youngest chil-dren have trouble planting, but we all pitch in.

Sally M. Hunter

As grandparents, we want the children to experience the beauty and richness of the earth. We are blessed by the earth when we pick a beautiful crop of Hochunk corn. And we are blessed with a beautiful family of Hochunk children.

—Sally M. Hunter

7

On a winter morning in St. Paul, Minnesota, Russell snuggles under his blanket. Outside, falling snow softly covers the houses, cars, and streets. The snowy street is quiet and peaceful. Suddenly, the alarm clock shrieks. Russell reaches out to push the snooze alarm, then wiggles back under his blanket.

It is *Wee-da-johow-hee-wee-dda,* January, the middle of winter. In the winter, plants and animals sleep and the cornfields rest under a blanket of snow. But not Russell—he can't sleep all day. He has to go to school. When the alarm rings again, Russell is up and on his way. He has hockey practice tonight, so he slings his equipment bag over his shoulder. Outside, he hurries through the new snow.

8

Russell is in the seventh grade. He loves to work on the computers in his school's math lab. Russell's family believes school is important, so he works hard in his classes. Since he also practices hockey after school in the winter, he's always busy.

Russell is 12 years old and has a mixed heritage of Winnebago, Creek, and Seminole Indian and French. His Winnebago grandfather is from the Winnebago reservation in the northeast corner of Nebraska. He lives near Russell in St. Paul now. Russell knows that his grandfather—called his *Choka* in the Winnebago language—is very proud of him. His Choka loves to watch Russell play football and hockey, and Russell helps his Choka and *Nookoo* during the seasons of corn. *(Nookoo* is short for *Nokomis,* the Ojibway word for grandmother. Russell's grandmother is Ojibway.)

Russell and his grandfather

The Winnebago people learned long ago how to grow and dry corn to preserve it, so that people would have food to eat all year long. Russell's great-grandmother taught her grandchildren the Winnebago traditions, and the family still continues these customs in the city. The Winnebago, who call themselves the Hochunk, listen to their elders to learn how to grow and dry corn.

Have you ever had sweet corn at a barbecue or a Fourth of July picnic? This popular yellow vegetable is just one kind of corn. There are many kinds and colors of corn. The corn that Russell's family grows and preserves has many different colors of kernels: blue, white, yellow, red, purple, and black. This kind of corn is called flint corn. It's also referred to as decorative corn or Indian corn. People often hang ears of this bright corn on the door as a decoration.

Corn, or maize, was first grown by the Native people of America thousands of years ago. Scientists found tiny corncobs in Central America that are about 7,000 years old. In North America, corn was grown more than 5,000 years ago. Scientists found corn in Bat Cave, New Mexico, that dates back to 3500 B.C. By A.D. 1500, Native people across America were growing corn on many kinds of land, from the swamps of Central America to the deserts of the southwestern United States to the fields south and east of the Great Lakes. Hochunk people grew corn in their homelands near Lake Michigan in Wisconsin.

Native Americans shared the gift of corn with the Europeans who came to America. From America corn made its way across the world. Now corn grows almost everywhere. People in the Americas, Europe, Africa, and Asia eat corn and use it to feed their animals. After wheat, corn is the second most important grain in the world. These grains, along with rice, form the main part of the human diet. In the United States, the world's leading producer of corn, corn is the most important crop.

*I*t is late spring. The snow has melted, the air is warm, and the birds are building nests. It is *My-dda-oo-nee-wee-dda*— June, the cultivating moon. Russell is expecting a phone call from his Choka. It is time to plant the corn. When Choka calls, he tells Russell to get ready for a trip to the farm. Russell imagines how it will feel when he is walking on the soft, plowed soil at the farm.

On a bright spring day, Russell, his mom, his two sisters, one younger brother, two cousins, an uncle, an aunt (called *Chu-wi* in the Hochunk language), and his grandparents travel south to a friend's farm. The trip in Choka's van is long for the younger children. To make the trip fun, the little kids play car games and the older children listen to music. Sometimes the kids fight, but the adults keep the peace.

13

The farmer, William Reiter, is of German heritage. His brother worked with Choka many years ago, and the two families are still good friends. William owns a large farm, where he grows corn and soybeans to sell. He shares part of one field with Russell's family. He has already plowed the ground, so it is ready to be planted. Each year the corn is planted in a different part of the field. This gives the soil a rest and allows time for the nutrients that were used up by last year's corn plants to be replaced.

Russell's grandfather, John, talks with William, the farmer.

Like other plants, the corn plant grows by using the earth's nutrients. Long ago, Choka tells Russell, Native people learned to plant crops in a new area each year so the plants would have fresh soil. The people allowed fields to lie fallow, or rest. They also knew how to fertilize the earth. Sometimes Hochunk people buried a dead fish under corn plants and other vegetable plants, which made the soil rich in nutrients.

Native people developed many kinds of corn. It is important to have many varieties of a plant so that if one type of corn plant gets a disease, the disease will not spread through all of the world's corn. Different corn plants do not get the same diseases, and they are not attacked by the same insects. Different plants have different protections.

15

Russell and his grandfather say a prayer for a good harvest of corn. They place tobacco on the ground as an offering to the Creator. In the past, the people depended on the corn crop for their survival. They prayed and gave offerings of tobacco in the hope of getting a good harvest. Corn is valued as a traditional "food of life." It is called the "staff of life," which means it supports life. People lean on a staff to walk, just as they lean on or depend on corn to live.

Corn is not only a basic food source for Hochunk people, but it also has a spiritual meaning. The elders of the tribe tell a special story about corn. They say it was a gift from the spirits.

The elders explain that when the Hochunk people had a problem or needed something, they fasted (went without food), and they prayed. They got ideas and inspiration from praying and fasting. Often the person who fasted had a dream in which a person or spirit appeared with some knowledge. The Hochunk people learned many things from their dreams and visions. For example, the people learned how to make birchbark canoes, flutes, and ceremonial whistles. The drum that Hochunk singers use came in the form of a person. Someone had a dream about that.

The elders tell a story about the leader of a family clan who fasted for his people. The clan leader was the one who fasted, because the leader did not want the others to have to suffer the hardship of fasting. Fasting is very difficult. This was a kindness that the clan leader could do for his people. Kindness toward others is a strong Hochunk value.

The clan leader was fasting, and a spirit appeared in his dream. The spirit was the Corn Person, who told him exactly what to do to plant, grow, and preserve corn so his people would have a delicious grain to eat. The Corn Person showed the clan leader how to plant the corn by digging a hole in a small mound of soil and putting the corn seed in the ground. When the corn grew, the Corn Person told the clan leader how to care for the plants and when it was time to pick the corn.

Russell helps his Choka hoe straight rows in the field where they are planting the corn. Russell uses math to carefully measure rows and plant the hard, dry seeds. The seeds are corn kernels that have been allowed to dry out. The rows are measured 12 inches apart. Russell plants a few seeds every 18 inches. This gives the plants enough room to grow. Russell's Choka smiles and teases him, saying that Russell is better with a hockey stick than he is with the gardening hoe.

Russell hoes the earth in preparation for planting the corn.

Russell's sisters, Andrea and Rachel, and his brother Chebon (*Chebon* means "boy" in the Creek language), are busy helping with the planting. They get down on their knees in the dirt and scrape the soil with their fingers. Russell's cousin Jessica and his uncle John are hoeing, too. Others are measuring rows. Each kernel is placed gently in the earth.

Andrea and Rachel plant corn seeds.

19

The soil around the seeds should be wet for the planting. Since the soil is dry today, Russell's mother and sister bring water in buckets. When Rachel and Chebon are finished with their part of the work, they play on the swing, going higher and higher and laughing in the spring morning. The sweet smells of lilac blossoms and fresh grass fill the air.

After the corn seeds are planted, they must be watered. Later, when the young plants have sprouted, they must be weeded and tended until they are fully grown and ready for harvest.

The soil is quite dry and must be watered.

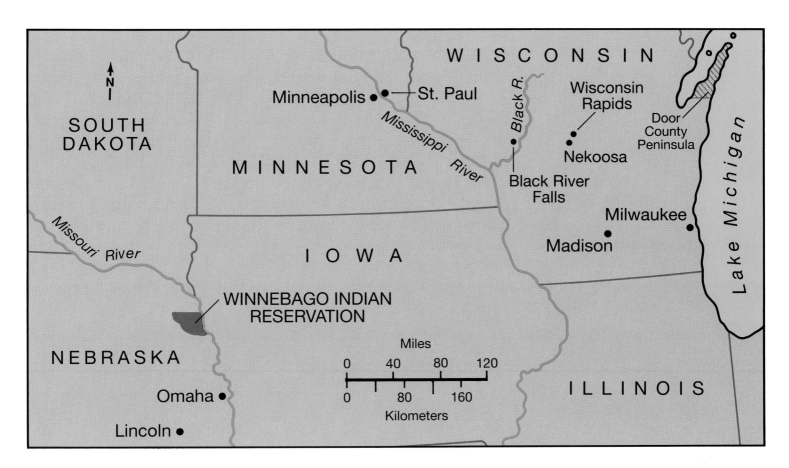

The map shows the following labels:

WISCONSIN
SOUTH DAKOTA
MINNESOTA
IOWA
NEBRASKA
ILLINOIS
Minneapolis
St. Paul
Wisconsin Rapids
Door County Peninsula
Nekoosa
Black River Falls
Milwaukee
Madison
Omaha
Lincoln
WINNEBAGO INDIAN RESERVATION
Missouri River
Mississippi River
Black R.
Lake Michigan

Miles
0 40 80 120
0 80 160
Kilometers

The Hochunk homelands are near Door County, Wisconsin, and in the area around Nekoosa. Many Hochunk people also live in Nebraska, where the Winnebago reservation is.

On the trip back to the city, Choka tells the story of how Hochunk people hunted for food and grew corn in Wisconsin long ago. The people originally came from near Door County Peninsula in northern Wisconsin (Red Banks of Green Bay). In the 1830s, the Winnebagos had to give up their land to the United States government. They were moved to Minnesota, then to South Dakota, and finally to Nebraska. Many Winnebago people still live in Nebraska. Others stayed or returned to south central Wisconsin, where they grew corn.

21

The Hochunk had summer vegetable gardens and grew corn to eat throughout the year. The people also hunted game and collected the fruits and vegetables that grew wild in the forest areas near the Great Lakes. Many Hochunk people continue to plant and grow corn, but they get most of their food from supermarkets or restaurants.

As Russell's family nears the city, Choka decides to treat his grandchildren to supper at a favorite restaurant. Russell is hungry and happy to stop on the way home for burgers and french fries.

With care, these corn seeds will grow into healthy plants.

*T*he next time Russell visits the farm, it is July, called *Wa-xoch-wee-dda,* or the corn tasseling moon. When the weather is hot, the corn grows tall. So do the weeds. Russell and his sister Andrea are going to the farm with Choka and Nookoo to weed the corn. Russell feels very warm and sticky and hopes there will be a breeze on the farm.

By pulling out the weeds that pop up near the corn plants, people help the corn. The plants will have enough room to grow, without being choked by the weeds. The elders say corn is a relative and the weeds must be removed so they do not strangle our relative. Russell and Andrea also clean the cornstalks by pulling off any leaves on the lower part of the stems. These leaves are called "suckers," and they take away some of the plant's growing power.

Hochunk people understand that all living things are connected and depend upon one another, just as people depend on one another for many things. We must respect plants and animals, the earth and all living things, because they are our relatives. Choka tells Russell to remember that people need corn and corn needs people.

Corn does not grow on its own as a wild plant. The kernels of the corn plant do not scatter and grow into new plants. Instead, corn must be cultivated. People must plant the seeds, fertilize the soil, and care for the corn plant.

Russell looks carefully at the corn. The stalks shoot up fast—they are already very tall. Corn is a grass, part of the same grain family as rice, wheat, oats, barley, and rye. Leaves grow from joints in the stalks called nodes. Corn husks sprout from the nodes. Inside the wrapped leaves of the husks, hundreds of kernels of corn will grow on ears. The kernels are not yet mature. They are a light, clear white now, but later they will turn many colors.

*I*n the fall, the corn is ripe and ready for harvest. It is late August, *Wee-da-jox-hee-wee-dda,* or the corn popping moon. When the cornstalks begin to dry, becoming yellow in the sun, the farmer checks the corn kernels. If they are white and milky in the center, the time has come to harvest the corn. This is a big job, and all the family members share the work.

25

Russell is starting the eighth grade. Football season has begun. After watching Russell play football, Choka reminds him that the family will be bringing the corn home this weekend and that he needs Russell to help with the harvest. Russell is glad there are no football games on the weekend, so he can go with his family for the corn harvest.

Once again the family travels to the farm. This time they bring a trailer for carrying the harvest home to the city. On the farm, the children can ride in the cornfields on the trailer. It's great fun.

Russell is a running back on his school football team.

Everyone in the family pitches in to harvest the corn.

When they arrive at the farm, Chebon chases the younger kids into the tall corn. Soon everyone starts pulling husks of corn from the stalks. Everyone has a job to do. The youngest kids empty the full pails of corn into the trailer. The older children find the ears of corn on the stalks and pull them off with a jerk or twist. Russell gets scratches on his bare arms as he works. He wishes he had worn a long-sleeved shirt. Russell's aunt and uncle tease him to make him laugh and make the work fun. Rachel is surprised to find a tiny melon growing in the middle of a row of corn.

27

After three hours, the trailer is filled with ripe corn. The children sit in the trailer on top of the corn as they drive away from the harvested cornfield.

Back at the house in St. Paul, Russell helps unload the trailer. He piles the ears of corn into a wheelbarrow and dumps them onto a plastic tarp in the backyard. Now the family prepares the corn to be dried. First they pull off the husks that cover the ears of corn. Then Nookoo boils the corn on the cob on her stove for eight minutes. This is called blanching the corn. Nookoo carries bowls of hot corn on the cob outside to cool. Ouch! Rachel picked up a hot corncob before it was cool enough to touch. It stings for a minute, then she is fine.

Family members unload the corn harvest from the trailer.

When the corn has cooled, each kernel is separated from the cob with a spoon. Choka explains that in the past the Hochunk people used clamshells instead of spoons to separate the kernels. The clamshells, which were gathered from lakes and streams, worked well because they were thin and sharp and could reach between the kernels. Modern metal spoons work pretty well, too.

Each kernel must be taken from the cob carefully so that the heart—the place where the kernel connects to the cob—is not lost. The heart has the best flavor.

Left: *The family husks the corn in the backyard, then Nookoo boils it.* Opposite: *The kernels are carefully removed from the ears of corn.*

The boiled corn is spread out on screens to dry.

Under the big oak trees in the backyard, the family members sit together in a circle of chairs. They fill pans of all sizes with the corn kernels and throw away the empty corncobs in garbage pails. Chu-wi (Russell's aunt) and the children laugh at the kernels that sometimes bounce out of the pans as if they have a mind of their own. Instead of complaining about the hard work, everyone talks and laughs.

After the corn kernels are removed from the cobs, the drying process begins. Russell's hands are sticky, and he notices the smell of wet corn all around him, like opening a can of corn, only much stronger. Pans full of corn are carried to drying screens, where the wet kernels are spread in the sun to dry. Rachel reaches up to smooth the kernels with her hands. The layers must be thin so that no moisture stays in the corn. Nookoo will turn the corn kernels often to make sure they dry out completely. Moisture can cause the corn to get moldy, and it could spoil. If the weather is hot and dry, the corn will dry out in three days.

Sometimes Nookoo dries the corn in the house on an oil-cloth (a kind of waterproof cloth). She uses two fans to blow air across the thin layer of kernels. Many Native people find new ways of doing old things. By drying the corn in the house with fans, the job can be done even in wet weather. Doing it this way takes five days. Corn can also be dried in an oven in one day, but some people say it is not as delicious as corn that dries slowly.

When the corn dries outside, the wind winnows, or cleans, the kernels by blowing away the bits of tassels, husks, and chaff (seed coverings, or hulls) that cling to them. Inside, fans do the winnowing.

When the corn is very dry, it is stored in glass jars on shelves for the winter. Nookoo and Choka share the corn with family and others who would like to use it for a dinner or gathering.

Later in the fall, all the relatives gather together for a big dinner to celebrate the corn harvest. Russell closes his eyes to pray with his family at the table. The dinner is a time to say thank you to the earth and to the Creator for providing a good corn season.

Indian Corn Soup

Hochunk people serve this soup as an expression of thanks-giving to the Creator. This soup is also served during naming ceremonies (when babies are named), funerals, weddings, or whenever there is a traditional feast and gathering of the people.

Corn: Use three quarts of dried, winnowed Indian corn. (Indian corn is the multicolored corn—yellow, blue, red, purple, white.) Wash it in small portions to remove any tassels or hulls.

Water: For boiling the corn, use ten quarts of water for three quarts of corn. The water will boil off, so add more hot water to make the soup as thin or thick as you want. Watch carefully as the corn boils so it doesn't stick to the kettle. Boil the corn for eight hours, stirring frequently.

Meat: Cut four pounds of beef or venison into small pieces and add the meat to the corn and water after the corn has boiled for four hours. Salt to taste while cooking. If you want a richer soup, add beef broth.

There should always be enough water in the pot to cover all the meat and the corn. Watch and stir the soup often to keep the corn from burning.

There are many ways to cook and eat corn. Native people grind it into a flour to make bread, tamales, and tortillas. Some people make a flat, delicate cornbread from grated corn off the cob, and others remove the hulls of the kernels and boil them to make hominy. There's also corn on the cob, popcorn, and Winnebago corn soup.

To make the traditional corn soup, Nookoo boils dried corn all day on the stove in venison broth. Russell loves corn soup and asks for seconds.

Another way Hochunk people celebrate the corn harvest is with a dance. Every fall a dance is held in Black River Falls, Wisconsin. The people, including elders and tiny tots, bring their dance clothes for the powwow. The men and boys wear headpieces made of deer tail hairs and porcupine hair. The women wear glass bead necklaces and dresses decorated with ribbon designs. Powwows are dances that are celebrations. They include prayers and songs that pay special honor to someone.

Russell and his family drive to Black River Falls for the powwow, and they also dance at the Winnebago powwow in Nebraska. They dance the Green Corn Dance. Partners dance together in a shuffle-type step. Everyone can participate, even the children. The dancers make a double line with their partners, following the leading couple around the powwow arena.

Russell's grandmother helps him get ready for the Green Corn Dance at the powwow.

The Green Corn Dance is a short form of a ceremonial dance that predicted a good harvest or celebrated a good harvest. The dance may continue through several songs and last up to 45 minutes or more, depending on how many songs are sung. Sometimes the songs tell the dancers to move backward or forward. Russell has a lot of fun doing the Green Corn Dance.

The powwow completes the circle of the corn seasons. Soon snow will cover the earth once more. When the cornfields are resting under a blanket of snow, Russell will wait for Choka to call, and once again he will help his family during the four seasons of corn.

Word List

chaff—seed coverings, or hulls

clan—a group of people united by ancestry

fast—to choose to go without food

Hochunk—Indian people from Wisconsin and Nebraska, sometimes called Winnebago.

hominy—corn that has been soaked in a solution and boiled so that the hulls separate from the kernels

hull—the outer covering of a kernel of corn

husk—the outer covering of an ear of corn

maize—corn. In the United States, most people refer to maize as "corn," but in Europe and England, the word *corn* means grain and *maize* is the word for corn.

Nokomis—Ojibway word for grandmother

Nookoo—nickname or abbreviation of "Nokomis"

powwow—a celebration of Indian culture that includes dancing, prayers, and drumming

tassel—the male flower of the corn plant, which grows at the top of the stalk and produces pollen

Winnebago—name given by Europeans to Indian people from Wisconsin and Nebraska; the word they use to refer to themselves is *Hochunk.*

winnow—to separate any extra material from the kernels of corn

Hochunk Words

Choka (CHOH kah)—grandfather

Chu-wi (CHEW wee)—aunt

My-dda-oo-nee-wee-dda (my dah ooh nee wee dah)—June, the cultivating moon

Wa-xoch-wee-dda (wah hoe-ch wee dah)—July, the corn tasseling moon

Wee-da-johow-hee-wee-dda (wee DAH joh oh hee wee dah)—January, the middle of winter moon

Wee-da-jox-hee-wee-dda (wee DAH joh hee wee dah)—August, the corn popping moon

The names of the seasons are:

Winter—**Mah-nee**

Spring—**Wah-na**

Summer—**Dok**

Fall—**Chah-nee**

For Further Reading

Aliki. *Corn Is Maize: The Gift of the Indians.* New York: Thomas Y. Crowell, 1976.

People of Corn: A Mayan Story. Retold by Mary-Joan Gerson. Pictures by Carla Golembe. Boston: Little, Brown & Co., 1995.

Peters, Russell M. *Clambake: A Wampanoag Tradition.* Minneapolis: Lerner Publications, 1992.

Regguinti, Gordon. *The Sacred Harvest: Ojibway Wild Rice Gathering.* Minneapolis: Lerner Publications, 1992.